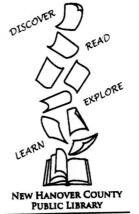

NEW HANOVER COUNTY PUBLIC LIBRARY

If found, please return to:
201 Chestnut St.
Wilmington, NC 28401
(910) 798-6300
http://www.nhclibrary.org

WHEN THE MEN
GO OFF TO WAR

WHEN THE MEN
GO OFF TO WAR

POEMS
VICTORIA KELLY

NAVAL INSTITUTE PRESS
ANNAPOLIS, MARYLAND

Naval Institute Press
291 Wood Road
Annapolis, MD 21402

Library of Congress Cataloging-in-Publication Data
Kelly, Victoria.
  [Poems Selections]
  When the men go off to war : poems / Victoria Kelly.
     pages cm
  ISBN 978-1-61251-904-3 (alk. paper) — ISBN 978-1-61251-
905-0 (ebook)
  I. Title.
  PS3611.E4575A6 2015
  811'.6—dc23

                                                   2015015113

♾ Print editions meet the requirements of ANSI/NISO z39.48-
1992 (Permanence of Paper).
Printed in the United States of America.

23 22 21 20 19 18 17 16 15   9 8 7 6 5 4 3 2 1
First printing

FOR WILL

Contents

PART ONE

DEPARTURE

When the Men Go Off to War

What happens when they leave
is that the houses fold up like paper dolls,
the children roll up their socks and sweaters
and tuck the dogs into little black suitcases.
Across the street the trees are unrooting,
the mailboxes rising up like dandelion stems,
and eventually we too float off,
the houses tucked neatly inside our purses, and the children
tumbling gleefully after us,
and beneath us the base has disappeared, the rows
of pink houses all the way to the ocean—gone,
and the whole city has slipped off the white earth
like a table being cleared for lunch.

We set up for a few weeks at a time
in places like Estonia or Laos—
places where they still have legends,
where a town of women appearing in the middle of the night
is surprising but not unheard of. The locals come to watch
our strange carnival unpacking in some wheat field
outside Paldiski—we invite them in for coffee,
forgetting for a minute
that some of our own men won't come home again;
and sometimes, a wife or two won't either.
She'll meet someone else, say, and
it's one of those things we don't talk about,
how people fall in and out of love—
and also, what the chaplains are for.

And then, a few days before the planes fly in,
we return. We roll out the sidewalks and make the beds,
tether the trees to the yard.
On the airfield, everything is as it should be—
our matte red lipstick, the babies blanketed inside strollers.

Only, our husbands look at us a little sadly,
the way people do when they know
they have changed but don't want to say it.
Instead they say, What have you been doing all this time?
And we say, Oh you know, the dishes,
and they laugh and say,
Thank God some things stay the same.

THE HOTEL

We lived by the ocean, next to an old hotel
where ladies went when "summer" was still
a verb—to play croquet, to get married. Eighty
years ago a rich man jumped from a sixth-floor
window; now there are rumors of ghosts, of bellhops

who appear in the stairwell, warning guests away.
One night in winter, when the hotel was closed,
we found ourselves in the lobby, drunk and tired,
and crept along the corridor imagining the paint
when it was slick and there were men in smoking

jackets milling about after dinner. They didn't know
what was coming, did they, those beautiful travelers—
waiting for wives to sign their perfumed letters
before descending to the ballroom, the glass doors
flung open toward the sea and the salt air pungent as

wild roses. How magnificent it must have been
to have waltzed with Fitzgerald past the gift shop,
the barber shop, the radio station broadcasting Lindbergh
as he flew by—to have danced straight to the precipice
of the Depression, before the pools were drained and

the tennis courts closed and the caulk on the bathtubs
began to yellow. How merciful to be unaware, for a night,
that one is condemned to dance forever somewhere
between this world and the next—a dusky spectacle
for drunken tourists who wait anxiously for the rustle
of an old silk gown, the thrill of a shiver up their spines.

Watching from the Runway
A Cento*

This is a war:
It is a lost road into the air,
voices just audible above the drone.
One by one they appear in
the falling light
with grave, uplifted faces,
climb on sketchy ladders toward God
and strike out at the air,
the promise of the appalling air,
to disappear from sight behind the sun.

This is the hour that writers eulogize.
And we have become beautiful without even knowing it,
and stand to wave farewell from our
several-inch-high cars and trucks,
left to think about what's going to happen to them.

Here there is still the backstage quiet,

and in every house in heaven there are lights waving,

and under the new and terrible rules of romance

we never dreamed it could be like this,

the tremolo of their brightness: light

fading through the darkness like a sigh.

I do not see eternity,

only

a million ordinary mornings,

the glittering neutrality,

the hours we gathered in our hands, and then let fall.

*Sources: Randall Jarrell, "Eighth Air Force," line 11; Donald Hall, "An Airstrip in Essex," line 1; Natasha Trethewey, "Pastoral," line 9; Thom Gunn, "My Sad Captains," line 1; Linda McCarriston, "Riding out at Evening," line 22; William Jay Smith, "Galileo Galilei," line 18; John Ormond, "Cathedral Builders," line 1; David Wagoner, "The Nesting Ground," line 14; Philip Levine, "For Fran," line 16; Howard Nemerov, "Runes," line 27; Jehanne Dubrow, "O' Dark Hundred," line 1; Billy Collins, "Nightclub," line 46; Barbara Howes, "The Nudist Colony," line 34; Maxine Kumin, "Highway Hypothesis," line 7; Kenneth Patchen, "The Little Green Blackbird," line 70; Sharon Olds, "Ideographs," line 25; W. S. Merwin, "In the Night Fields," line 14; Reed Whittemore, "Reflections upon a Recurrent Suggestion by Civil Defense Authorities that I Build a Bombshelter in My Backyard," line 16; George Bilgere, "The Ineffable," line 26; Henry Rago, "The Knowledge of Light," line 5; Henri Coulette, "Intaglio," line 41; Lawrence Ferlinghetti, "New York–Albany," line 51; Victoria Kelly, "Watching from the Runway," line 23; John Malcolm Brinnin, "Hotel Paradiso e Commerciale," line 45; James Merrill, "The Country of a Thousand Years of Peace," line 9; Richmond Lattimore, "Anniversary," line 7.

THE GOOD WIFE BEFORE DEPLOYMENT

Really, it is a slow, agonized departure,
ruinous as an argument in a rainstorm:
the Corvette stalled on the highway
and my husband's fist against the dashboard,
while he tells me this is never how he saw it—
the townhouse, the yellow dog, me.
A policeman knocks on the window;
he is hunched against the black night, like a soldier himself.
And I know a good wife would understand,
a good wife would know her husband
is afraid of her and God;
he is afraid of having something to lose.

The Messengers

How can you help
picturing it,
the small huddle on your doorstep—
the commander; the priest who married you;
the women with their sad, drawn faces.
You know
the only message you will get
from the pink, blistered mountains of Kabul
is the one that comes when you're thinking about the dishes
or out buying oranges.
And how can you not see
the faces of these people
in every housewife or postman who pauses
at the edge of your driveway;
even the sack of letters, the dog pawing at the lawn
won't stop you from sleeping
with the bedside light on.

LESSONS

There is a certain way to fold the shirt of a military man;
a certain way to wash a flight suit; certain rules to follow

at a dining-out (*thou shalt not murder the Queen's English*);
a certain way to tell a Super Hornet from a Hornet; a certain

protocol for the phone chain; certain shoes to wear
on an aircraft carrier; certain magazines you cannot mail abroad;

certain wives who can't keep a secret; certain husbands whose secrets
your husband told you. These are things they don't teach you

in public school, or at Harvard—you can read Chaucer but not the bars
on a uniform, and you will never understand the acronyms

of a weather report, or a flight schedule. Certainly, after the first thrills
of domesticity, you never expected the loneliness, the certainty

of homelessness—or any of those long gray afternoons
by the ocean in winter, waiting for the laundry to dry.

PATUXENT RIVER

We drove the back roads toward the base,
the luggage stacked in the trunk and the dog
howling from the backseat. My husband
stopped the car, stepped out to the road, and lifted
his face toward the roar of the jets overhead, looking
the way people look in the rain in movies
when they are happy. To him they were
as beautiful as children, those gray,
hairless beasts that had brought us here,
but he talked of them like mistresses, and he loved them,
and I loved him, and we stood there between the
farms and the lights of the Chinese restaurant,
the lives behind those windows pulsing
like the chests of a hundred tiny birds, but I could see

this life would be smaller than the last—there was
only the one highway, after all, a few motels, a diner,
and through the trees a small white church
with scarred stone stairs, like the ones
my grandmother stands on in her wedding pictures.
She had a small life too,
her needlepoint and the tidy compartments
of her mind that would be closed off in widowhood,
one by one, like the rooms of a half-used manor.
But in that moment, the roses of her bouquet fresh
as milk and my grandfather's fingers wrapped
around her waist, perhaps
she saw everything, all the way through
to my own glittering February night, when I would stand
under the bellies of those planes, their scarlet flares of light,
thinking of her.

Planning

In the bathroom, fingering the wheel of tiny blue pills, you know that in a month he'll be deployed and gone for eight more after that, but there is Dubai in August if the flights are cheap, the dripping heat and those cream hotel sheets, and three months later if he comes home you might be in California, some desert town where they say the hospitals aren't good and the air is bad for children, but if it isn't California it will be Texas and either way the sun will be hot and red and the nights very cold, and you'll be far from your parents who are aging, walking hesitantly now like toddlers, and either way you'll have to sell the house by the ocean you've come to love so much, the jets roaring in like lions, and inside every cockpit somebody's beloved daughter or somebody's beloved son coming back to life.

REVERIE ON LEAVE

Walking the city at night we found a carousel
lit with pink light, the painted horses old
as wooden toys. It is true: there are places
you can only reach on the back of a horse—
sometimes, when the music speeds up,
the spell of life lifts,
and there's that gray dog you loved, that uncle,
and your parents haven't come yet but
their own parents are waiting for them
by a pool, sipping pineapple juice, looking
nothing like you last saw them, when they were rigid
and still, their faces caked with makeup.
Your grandmother
leans into a lawn chair, because there is
no hurry, you are never too old
to be young here. Always, more are arriving,
emerging dreamily
from the water, touching their faces and reaching
for useless things—glasses, watches,
the hands of people they left behind
the curtain. My God, how close they all seem,
how real—
until the city slows down and
the horses turn back
to plaster and brass, while in the courtyard,
the ticket taker yawns into his shirt sleeve
and wraps coins in brown cardboard tubes.

THE BEAUTIFUL SADNESS

A friend joked she should hire an assistant
in Delhi to answer her mother's hostile, drunken
e-mails: *Bountiful Greetings*, the responses would begin,
I have received your lovely note. And we stood there

imagining flowers bright as wax and the green wings
of insects and saris drying in the window; but perhaps,
in another room of that house, there was a bed
with the assistant's sleeping mother, whose feet,
tiny as a ballerina's, would not walk again, and when

the doctor puts a mask over my mouth, before I sleep,
before the fetus is gone, and my husband is called
back to base, I understand that these are all just parts
of the beautiful sadness, that in the clarity of grief
we can see all kinds of things, we can see, for once,

how death might be as unalarming as stepping onto a train,
the destination not terrible or romantic, just pleasant
as a carousel ride on a blue afternoon, the scratchy music
and the painted horses and familiar faces laughing
with their mouths turned into the wind.

HOTEL CIPRIANI

In Venice the escorts wore gold bikinis
and high heels by the side of the pool. I was
twenty and they were beautiful; my God, how
I envied their waists and long hair.
I didn't think about the old men or
whether they had mothers, only watched
them slip like jewels into the water, pink
arms arched like pianists', those diamond
bracelets like chains around their wrists.

QUANTUM THEORY

Fifty years ago, in Catholic school,
a nun gave my mother a ribbon
said to have been touched by a saint.
This was when her brother was still alive,
and masses were still said in Latin,
and people still wandered across the street
to other people's houses in the evening.

Now the school is coming down, and, six blocks away,
my grandmother forgets to brush her teeth.
The years are upon her, but they say
there are moments that go on forever—
somewhere else, on another plane.
If it is true
I wonder if somewhere out there,
my mother is still being given that ribbon,
and my uncle is waiting for her in the hallway
with his coat slung over his shoulder.
The sun is going down.
They are about to walk home,
and neither of them knows yet
about the cancer, or the laymen's masses,
or the war that is looming.
She is going to show him the ribbon
and they will believe it is real.

THE DEPARTURE

My dad dreamed he saw his dead father in the driveway, leaning against the hood of the red Jaguar they sold in 1966. Dad thought Grandpa had come for him, but he turned to see my grandmother bounding down the porch steps, purseless, her skirt bunched in her hands. She hadn't run in years. My grandfather held out his hand, and my father watched as they climbed into the car, waving at him like a couple of kids after a wedding. Two days later, in the waking world, my grandmother was taken to the hospital, and the whole time she was dying she was looking over our shoulders at something in the corner of the room. It occurred to me that my father, like his father and mother before him, used to say, *Someday when I'm older* . . . but then got old, and that everyone who has aged out of our lives might still be getting older somewhere else, blowing candles and breaking piñatas and making the crazy plans of people with all the time in the world.

Standing on the Airfield, before War

If there is one thing I should say before you go,
it should not be about standing on some driveway in Pensacola,
baptized by airplanes.

It should not be that the house was bare and there
was no food, but that we were young and the airplanes
were like tiny glass toys in the sky,
and there was all of it ahead of us then, there was
this whole life.

No, if there is only time in this goodbye
for one last affirmation,
let it not be of that pond blue summer, or letters
from home, or romance at all. Let it be of love when it's
more than this love, when it's not dazzling
or eager or brave—
like an old man before a party,
fixated on a tie, and his wife waiting
patiently in the kitchen, letting him decide.

PART TWO

ABSENCE

Homecoming

After my husband deployed, my brother got married.
The wedding was held in an old house called
Brentwood Manor, on Main Street in Morris Plains,
New Jersey. Around this house the city had been born—
the delis, the diners, the things I came to associate
with home—through the hedges, the Dunkin' Donuts,
the church that baptized me. These were the castles
I'd played in, and in the chairs fanning out around me
were all the characters of my childhood—
my old babysitter; my brother's football teammates;
the women from the PTA. Somehow they
had all emerged, aged, from those spent summers
into this one. We danced, the music spilled
into the street, some men walking home from the bars
sang Bruno Mars, and my brother's friend lit a joint
in the parking lot. "Where you been," he asked sleepily,
leaning against a lamppost. "Married," I said, and he
laughed. "Girl," he said, "married isn't a place,"
and through the window, under the gleaming lights
of the party, the guests held up their champagne.

Nights in the Gulf

I wish I knew you there,
a man curled up in a doll's bed and the tailhooks
pounding overhead and always
people up and down the stairs and
never enough hours, never enough quiet to last the night.

I wish I knew you over Kandahar,
the puckered smoke-black mountains
and the fire spitting at your tail, and the calls
coming in and going out and in those times,
or when it's over and you're making your way back,
I wonder if you come across angels while you're praying
for mail, see the faces of your grandparents
sliding past you in the dark.

Sometimes at night,
I walk to the beach where I took that last
photograph of you, remember how you worried
things would be different after so much time, that the dog
perhaps would not know you,
that this life you loved once
would just be one more thing to lose.

HARVARD REUNION

We were young still, only five years out,
so they housed us in a dorm on the far
corner of campus. It was a hot Boston June,
and there was no air conditioning in the building;
we shared deodorant as we dressed for dinner,
remembering the time we hitchhiked in miniskirts,
during a blizzard, to get to a party. We had stories
that had not been told in years. Walking through Harvard
Yard, we didn't recognize the students who lounged
on the steps of the library, waiting for graduation.
A Japanese tourist took our picture
sitting on those steps, then clapped his hands as if
we were performers in a tableau, actors who
went back to real life when the cameras were gone.
Really, when we graduated we got married, took pills,
bought dogs, got divorced. We desperately wanted
to be the kinds of people that tourist would think of
when he saw that photo again, years later, and wondered
what became of us. But you know,

we only managed to find ourselves
in the middle of ordinary summers—the heat
rising from the pavement like a prayer just sent,
like candle smoke in a quiet restaurant.

Almost

I can imagine living a whole life
in the house my parents almost bought in Morris Plains
across from the train station;
the way I almost played Red Light, Green Light
in that park next to the library
and almost went to school
at St. Virgil's Parish, on Speedwell Avenue;
the way my father almost made thirty years
of slow, moonlit walks to the station in winter,
my mother
waving from the kitchen window.
I can imagine growing up,
and almost taking the same train
to some publishing job in the city,
and coming home
to dinner with my parents next door,
to children who, on weekends,
almost hunt for clovers in the same park
I almost knew the name of once.

And how different
that life that barely passed me by
seems now
from this lonely, sunny afternoon at the beach
on some base in Virginia
under the brick-red blaze of summer—
the mothers fortified under hats and sunblock,
the tired children slowing down around me,
and a man
who could almost be my father
waving to the person behind me.

Unknown Numbers

He calls once in a while, the man
looking for his son. It's Dad, he insists,
his voice choked with age, but he has
the wrong number, and he can't hear
me; when I correct him he is disturbed.
I imagine him at a kitchen window, the film
of tears beginning; he is waiting for Dwayne
to appear under the streetlamp, a halo
of dark hair around his face. But it is late:
the dogs are whining and the houses are
filling up with light, and no one is emerging
from the dust.

    On the ship they also call
from unknown numbers, and my husband,
like Dwayne, is somewhere else; his voice
is far away, the words clipped by censors.
He is standing in some hallway, the hot
steam of sweat around him, and he
does not appear at my window either,
does not rap on the door, as if
he has just gone out to buy stamps
and forgotten his key.

To My Husband
Flying over Afghanistan
A Cento*

The pilot alone knows
the chill of closed eyelids
in the glaring white gap;
the wired minefield;
the stars in active orbit.
And all is from wreck, here, there—
the hot black dunes in the air.

Now I am safe in the deep V of a weekday;
how fibrous and incidental it all seems—
the Avon lady trekking door to door
the paper sacks stuffed full of oranges,
obscenely jewel-toned
while the whole cathedral crashes at your back.

*Sources: Andrew Joron, "Spine to Spin, Spoke to Speak," line 1; Marina Tsvetaeva, "Poems for Blok, 1," trans. Ilya Kaminsky and Jean Valentine, line 15; Medbh McGuckian, "Painting by Moonlight," line 12; Ciaran Carson, "Let Us Go Then," line 2; Marie Ponsot, "Imagining Starry" line 6; Gerard Manley Hopkins, "The Times Are Nightfall," line 6; Henri Cole, "Green Shade," line 5; Rachel Zucker, "After Baby after Baby," line 7; Sarah Gambito, "Holiday," line 17; David Trinidad, "9773 Comanche Ave.," line 10; Shin Yu Pai, "Six Persimmons," line 5; Joyelle McSweeney, "A Peacock in Spring," line 24; Kamau Brathwaite "Mesongs," line 5.

THE FUNERAL

On the night of your uncle's funeral, your mother tells you
how the priest drove the wrong way to the cemetery,
while both Aunt Sofia and the hearse turned right instead of left,
and when they finally met at the gravesite, the priest
got out of the car and started yelling at Aunt Sofia,
waving his hands and shouting, Why didn't you follow me,
because he was embarrassed, and Aunt Sofia cried and said something
in her Hungarian English, and later your father went up to the priest
and told him he should be ashamed, she was a woman
at her husband's funeral—and when it is all over, across the country,
you say the rosary for your uncle at your desk on base
with your work spread out in front of you, and your hands
run over the beads and over the papers but instead of Mary's face
all you can see is the priest, waving his arms in the cemetery,
and your uncle, how he would have laughed if he had been there.

Love Letters

For hundreds of years women have been writing to men
at war; our grandfathers kept letters inside combat boots,
wearing them thin as insect wings between fingertips,

and Josephine wrote, halfheartedly, to Napoleon while
he burned with love for her, and Georgia belles penned
wild, tragic letters in the wake of Sherman's march.

I wrote two hundred letters; they were not sad or long,
but I mailed them every afternoon from the post office
near the boardwalk. There were only three cashiers—

Cheryl, her wit sharp as glass; Manny,
who broke his leg that summer in Mexico;
and Dave, a Cambodian, who gave himself an American

name but never understood my city accent.
Sometimes I dreamed I was the daughter
of a small town, fifty years ago perhaps,

when all the young wives gathered, waiting for news
from men they had been kissing since the first grade.
But the sounds of the crowded beach brought me back

to this ocean, where a letter tossed into the waves off one
continent might be carried, by some miracle, to the waters
of another; or it might turn up, a lifetime from now, in some

swimming pool after a hurricane—the names long since
washed away, but some words still intact, the handwriting
startling in an age when no one writes by hand anymore

but wars still happen, and people still fall in love
with other people, and paper still falls through water
unhurriedly, like kings descending a stair.

How Emirati Women Shop

They pause by store windows, admiring
the gauzy yellow dresses. There are legions
of these women, cloaked in modesty, veiled
like brides. I picture their boudoirs, papered
in silk, a platter of figs on the nightstand, and
the black jewels between their thighs gleaming
like window glass. How unexpected, then, the
laughter in the ladies' room; how thrilling to
find the daughters of Scheherazade leaning
against the counter, careless as men, their black
hoods tossed over a chair. They are exquisite,
their lips perfectly red, their fingernails
tipped in pink. After they leave, there is only
the faint spice of their perfume. Centuries ago,
women here carried water, and babies; now
they carry their beauty, like plumage, under
their robes, the way rich men know they are most
powerful when no one knows exactly how rich
they are.

THOUGHTS OF A HIGH SCHOOL BOYFRIEND

The news came fast; his wife had died,
       eight months pregnant, his whole
                     life stolen
in an afternoon—the media outraged, the doctor tried
       for negligence. I saw his picture:
the family at the church, that boy I'd sworn to love, now twenty-nine
       and broken, the shine
of tears across his face. There was no scripture
       that could save him. He was alone.
I'd left him years ago; we fought,
    I tore his photograph and never thought
     he'd rise up in my dreams again—his young wife gone—
          caught in the agony of loss, the desperate prayers
          to return the ghosts that catch us unaware.

THE PRAYER FLAG

In a Kalona antique store, my husband
removes the flag from a basement shelf,
unfolds it, recognizes immediately the red
sun and black-inked prayers of someone's
long-perished son. What soldier it came by
we will never know, but we carry it in tissue
paper onto the wide Iowa streets, the way
some woman in Japan must have carried
that boy's name in the back of her throat;
and the way, in the middle of another long
war, I would carry my own dead child
inside me, through the glass hospital doors,
toward a sleep hard as a stone angel.

And this is how I know
that the same prayers of broken mothers
still float from this fragile earth, to all
those beautiful lives arranged above us
like paintings on a church ceiling.

PRAYERS OF AN AMERICAN WIFE

Two hours from Santiago by the Pato Piraña bus,
the cookie-makers hawk their *dulces* on the corner.
They hang their baskets on tree branches; they are tired
as men who stoop over workbenches all day.
In college, I stayed in a hotel near the square,
the sweet smell of *manjar* curled like a sleeping cat
in the back of every closet—while outside, the vendors
called prices to the children scrambling home for lunch.
I was so far from home.

   One day, three years into a marriage that took my husband
to another far ocean, I would dream back that too-bright place.
Another wives' club dinner, another *river-city* blackout,
and surely I know it all goes on somewhere still:
those white-eared dogs jumping at the trees;
the schoolgirls sitting cross-legged by the fountain,
teasing and flirting—though I imagine it's possible
the buses have long stopped coming,
the highway petering out one day a few miles from town,
and the black-capped drivers getting out at the end of the line
and scratching their heads, peering into the tall grass
where an old dirt road used to be.

On Sundays

On Sundays when I wake alone again
   to the dog's snoring, a day of keeping house,
the bells ringing from the church next door,
   I remember that we pray before different altars—
his a trembling ship at sea, a few lights in the rainy
   darkness, and out there he is not someone's spouse,
not someone's son, but someone far from here, at war.
   At home, things are not the way they were.
Sometimes I dream myself into an old life—
   a game of tag in the driveway, the cats sleeping
in the shade—there was always another hour
   for reading, always my mother laughing on the phone,
and so much time between child and wife,
   so many well-worn prayers for God to keep me.
But I knew things then I don't know now—
   that God was real, and I would never be alone.

THE STUDENT

She married young; her husband was a mechanic
on the same ship my husband was on,
somewhere in the Gulf of Oman. Every Tuesday,
she wrote him into the poems I assigned for class,
so that somehow this man managed
to do what my husband could not, to ascend
from the chaos of the carrier deck, the rancid stink
of the quarters underneath, into the little office on campus
where I graded my papers.

Two weeks before homecoming, her house was burglarized—
the bedroom ransacked, new curtains ripped down,
and all the pretty furniture coated
with the white dust the police left behind.
The response was clinical, the scene defiled,
like the corpses of strangers cut open in medical school.
I couldn't help wondering if the crime was an omen
of worse to come: that we would not know our husbands
when they returned, that the end would be nothing more
than a slow diminishing, like finely settled powder,
not sudden as a broken window, but ragged as the last breaths
of people when you are waiting for them to die,
when afterward all you will recover is a fingerprint,
faint as a ghost, on the bedside table.

BOUDOIR

One month before homecoming I had
my photograph taken in lingerie and eye shadow,
high heels bought at the mall, in a curtained
studio above a garage. I said one day I want
my husband to remember how thin I was, how long
my hair was, and you can see this in the photos,
that hubris laid bare—and my dark silhouette in the window
where I stood recalling the immaculate emptiness
after his departure, the way cleaning out the pantry
was like a thousand small deaths, every half-eaten box
of cereal like a shirt that might never be worn again.

PART THREE

HOMECOMING

ANNAPOLIS

When I met you, you were one
of a thousand blue-coated boys surging
through the gates on a Saturday night.
It was April but there was still a little
snow on the grass, and I was young enough
to think I was pretty but not so much
that I was troubled by it, or enabled.
Funny that I can't picture my shoes, only
the street underneath them—pitted like the rind
of an orange, worn down by a hundred thousand
young men just like you, midshipmen with
their covers tipped over their eyebrows,
each one knowing they will never belong
here more than they do now—for a few hours

the clatter of this liberty is theirs—because
it will never look the same as it does
on a Saturday night in April before curfew,
before June, before the President shakes
your hand and you are someone for a moment,
before the honeymoon and the arguments
of marriage, before carrier landings on dark
nights, before you're down in Afghanistan
and they want you dead, before the pageantry
of your homecoming, before wanting nothing
except to go back—to the war, yes, but maybe
you would keep going if you could, all the way
to the church, or that first flight in Pensacola,
or the crowded street where we were just kids
who knew nothing, except that there was more,
and it would certainly be everything
we dreamed of.

ATLANTIC CITY

In the forties my grandmother worshipped
sand as pale as Irish skin, the sirens
of casinos on summer afternoons.
One night, walking home from a dance,
a corsage red as a heart on her wrist,
she heard the footsteps of a man behind her,
    quick and slow, quick and slow.
These were the months of the boardwalk murders,
the curfews and pocketknives slipped into stockings,
but in the end she was saved by a gate—a latch
she knew and he did not—and a sprint to the front door,
while a neighbor's lights came on, yellow
as a cat's eyes in the dark.

In the fifties she married a man who drank
away the scalded bodies of Nagasaki, and
how many nights did she wake then to the rattle
of a latch in the yard, the footsteps
of a man at the edge of her bed,
so her daughter could have a daughter who
loved the ocean too but saw
the wreckage of a different war.

Kwansaba for a Wounded Warrior

Colin laughs and says he hasn't met
his wife yet among the nurses at
Brooke Army Med Center. "In Kunar, when
we were kicking off, and those hajjis
were flaming up the road, I wished
for any girl. But I'll tell you—
that was the baddest show on earth."

KEY WEST

People vanish, and turn up here:
on houseboats; in pizza shops; sipping
tequila on pink porches. The flying here is good,
he says, but that's not what keeps him coming back.
Hemingway knew it; my husband knows it too.
It's because he has become one
of the lost boys, here they are
no one's fathers and no one's sons, here they are
everything they wanted to be when they were children:
poets, pilots, cowboys swaddled in the orange light
of some dockside bar, and the whole island rocking gently
back and forth
back and forth.

HEROES

Sometimes you think it's hard to be a hero
these days, there are no wars
like the wars of your grandfather's days.

The truth is
so much of it now is just like life, the guys
coming over for a drink after work and the XO
breakdancing in a pair of running pants
at the Christmas party and all the lieutenants
in reindeer costumes with their girls on their arms,

and at the end of the night it is late and the dog is waiting
at the door and we could be just like any other couple,
stumbling home from any other party.

But when you talk about wartime, what you tell me
is how many stars there were, and how
some boys flew a kite on the mountain.
What you don't talk about
is huddling with a group of soldiers in a bunker
while the rockets came over the walls, how
most of you by chance came out, but two did not.
They were Canadian, you said offhandedly,
when you'd been home for a while,
and you never said it again.

Outside the Air Base

In the middle of rush hour traffic on
General Booth Boulevard, a homeless man
in army boots and a Panama hat darted into
the road by the 7-Eleven, just as the light
turned yellow.

We all slammed on our brakes.
One woman in a red Subaru skidded past him;
in the backseat, two girls in angel wings pressed
their noses to the window, and the man in the car
behind them leaned out to yell something none of us
could hear over the roar across the median.

Amid an explosion of horns, the man
looked up, startled, his lips
parting slightly, the teeth beneath yellow and worn
to nubs. His shirt was unbuttoned at the top;
we could make out the outline of a pair of dog tags
tattooed across his chest.

He was heavy in the middle, and gray, and it was strange,
but for a minute we could almost see him
the way he might have been forty years before, in the mud
in Khe Sanh, brave or trembling or thinking of some girl,
next to people we too might have known, people who had also been

brave or afraid, who came home or didn't, drank or didn't,
who fought or bought pit bulls or wrote poetry in the middle
of the night—

And then we were all back on General Booth Boulevard again,
thinking of dinner or library books or soccer practice,
and he was just a man in army boots patched over with duct tape

standing in the middle of the road. He paused,
then bent over slowly to retrieve a rock none of us saw;
it was the size of an artichoke, and he carried it
in the crook of his arm like a baby to the side
of the road, before smiling and waving us on.

ACCIDENTS

There is nothing like the sound
of a car hitting a tree, the stillness
when it is over. Blood thickens
the hair of the man inside,
his arms flung over the steering wheel as my husband
checks his pulse. The darkness lies like soot
over the scene, and no lights come on
in the neighbors' houses, there is only
the gray swell of engine smoke in the headlights,
the far blue lights of the ambulance we called.

The firemen drag their hoses onto the lawn,
help lift the bleeding man through a window
onto the stretcher.
Thank God you were here, one of them says,
turning toward us. It is remarkably quieter
than accidents on tv shows; no one yells
for bandages or water. In the bay
of the ambulance the man lifts his head
like someone just pulled from a pool,
like there is so much color, such endless
sky.

There is a feeling like fate to our passing by,
until a policeman takes our statements
for the court, laments that the man we saved
is a drunk driver, on bail. Suddenly, the hour
we lost seems important. It occurs to me that
this rescue
is a little like the war my husband just returned from:
you never know who you are supposed to save,
whether you would do it again
if you knew more; and which of these inclinations
makes you a good person, and which
will find you at night.

JOSEPHINE

Sometimes she sees her late husband
while she is getting dressed in the morning;
he is smoking perhaps or shoveling snow
in the Kansas winter, but mostly it is
her mother who flickers on the other side
of the room, as if pulled through a mirror—
that dark beauty who sang *La Bohème*
in the Italian opera, wore silk and took Milanese
lovers. They fled when the War came, took
nothing except the rosaries the nuns gave them,
and moved to Hollywood, where Josephine danced
in films with MGM and took her own place
on the periphery of fame. She is old now,
the heirlooms distributed, and the names of her
grandchildren escape her—but she had
some wild times, didn't she, that young thing
in the wanton spell of Rome, of California
when it was all orange groves and movie stars;
even now, she sees her girlhood in color, bright
as a parachute against the snow. In the morning
she laughs like a bride.

THE CRASH

Beside the highway, a tower of black smoke was rising
like a phoenix over the tree line. A dozen cars were parked
on the overpass, the drivers leaning over the railing
with their doors flung open. Getting out of my car,

I was knocked back by the smell; it was a smell I had known
only once in my life, standing on a hill in New Jersey
as the ash floated out of the City. But when I moved closer
to the side of the road, I could tell it was not a building on fire,

but some kind of airplane—and in the blare of the sirens
I couldn't hear what the woman next to me was saying, but
the car radio was saying it was a jet, a pilot had gone down
on Birdneck Road—and for a moment in the April glare,

I thought I could see my husband climbing over the edge
of the railing in his flight suit,
until my phone rang, and it was the skipper's wife
calling to say, *it wasn't one of ours, it wasn't one of ours*—

and only then did I turn back to the crowd,
all those people with their hands over their mouths,
and all I could think was how three minutes later
it might have been my car down there, and it might

have been my husband's plane, and what God is this
who stayed the union of our darkest imaginations?

ROCK CLIMBING

A friend took me rock climbing
when we were seventeen; it was spring
in New Jersey and the trees
were green as emeralds, and I stood alone in the woods
while he hooked the ropes to the top of the cliff and
rappelled down to meet me. There was no one around
for miles. We climbed to the top
of two hundred feet, and when we got there
he put his arm around my shoulder, and the whole county
was beneath us and we could see rivers like
blue ribbons disappearing over the edge of the earth.

Four days later I saw him on the news, lying on a precipice
of that same cliff, halfway to the bottom. The ropes
we had been using had snapped, he had broken
his back and his skull; a crew of paramedics
hauled him into the bay of a helicopter. In the hospital,
when he was awake, I asked him—desperate
for some kind of proof—if he had seen God
while he was lying there, worried about dying
and things like that; but he only shook
his head and told me not to be so provincial.

He walked in graduation with our class,
but afterward, we lost touch. Years later, I heard
he was still going back to those same cliffs, still
driving the highways of the town I'd left, but

I was different, I never climbed again, and I can only
see now, one deployment and a thousand prayers later,
how easy it is to say *things like that* don't happen
to people like us, when you know better, you really
know better.

Elegy

You know this: one day these days
will be over—this war and the lieutenants
you drank with, the perfumed Arabian
port calls and those blazing nights—
and perhaps you will think that you had not done
what you set out to do, you never killed one man
to save another, never saw a real dogfight,
and the war was almost over
when you got there; there will only be
a few brave moments to cling to,
a few faces in the street
to remind you
of some old friends.

But you should know this too: we never did have
the time of our lives. There is nothing
like the glory of someone's lost years, nothing
as poetic as the memory
of the glimmering, snow-lit streets of Annapolis,
or a thousand flags waving
for a plane coming home.

Ghosts

All through the pregnancy she is like a ghost,
half in this world and half in some other,
her body pale and shimmering as an oyster.
She moves the way we can sometimes feel people
brush against us long after they are gone, parading about
in their finest clothes perhaps, the grandmothers in their
pink hats and pointed shoes and the soldiers in
stiff dress blues. We can't see them but we know
they are there, dancing through the living room.
I imagine they can talk to her, my grandfather
explaining to my daughter what music is, how many
oranges there will be in summer. In the blaze of birth
he will be there too, flushed with color, though as she
grows up he will grow dimmer, blanching to the gray
of a photograph pasted in a cardboard wedding album.

THE GREEN FLASH

And on certain nights on palm-treed Cayman beaches,
   the renters wander out at sunset among the scattered
chairs, the half-buried sandwich crusts, all the clatter
   of the day gone, the babies glazed with sleep,

and all of us waiting for the sun to move. It's thought
   to sink into the water in a flash of green; we gather around
the few old men who've seen it, the kingfishers hovering
   too, like disciples, aware that more often than not,

you can't look at the sun head-on, like a lot of other things—
   your brother's anxious tics, say, or the war on tv. You wonder
what would change if you saw it, what would happen to you after;
   whether part of you—like the soul of some marooned conch, clinging
to its sea-crusted shell—would suddenly lift off, shudder
   free: rise up with the birds, toward some far empyrean rafter.

BIRTH

This kind of love is a winged thing:
    my husband with our daughter in his arms,
    the empty beach, the morning
    polished as citrine.
Now that she is here we will never be
    old again, daylight flickers on
    and she blinks,
    we think about breakfast and bills but
    she watches the birds,
    looks at us
    like there are no playgrounds,
    no princess parties, no boyfriends waiting
    by the gym at seventeen. She is only
    six weeks old and there are no other
    pleasures: everything is ageless here, everything
    is here.

INTO THE FRAY

At naptime she arranges her dolls like soldiers
in her crib and prepares them
for war. *Baba ta!* she cries, refusing sleep.
She waves one fat fist in the air,
grabs Meerkat by the tail. *Da sha didi*, she insists.
We will not surrender!

But something is amiss; she surveys her army, paces
the mattress with a frown. At last it is discovered—
Bunny has mutinied; such subversion cannot stand.
She throws him from the crib in triumph.
Now, she says, satisfied. We will rest
before the battle. And she lies down,
takes Duckling in her tiny arms, and draws him close.

The War Is Not Here

but planes still go down sometimes,
even on Wednesday mornings, even on this side
of the ocean, a dozen miles from the beach,
while an old man unwinds his kite and
some women are icing cakes in the church, because
the war is somewhere else and God knows
we only pray for soldiers on Sundays.

But what if someone you know—your husband, say—
happens to be flying when that jet goes down, and what if
he hears the guy on the radio and then he doesn't
hear him anymore and what if all he sees is the black
ripple of ocean spreading like tar and there is no way to move
all that water back, in fact there is only a moment to think
of the guy's mother, only a moment to call the helicopters
and the hospital, and what if this is not the war he trained for,
just an ordinary
morning flying—
is it heroism if no one drops a bomb or dives into the underbrush,
is it a story to sustain a man
when everything else falls away
except that beautiful splintered body rising from the waves,
that heartbeat coming back to drum another sixty years?

ORDINARY EVENINGS

Sometimes it is the old wars that catch us
off guard—during some Tuesday dinner
at a Japanese steakhouse, say, when the sweatered
man across the table describes how he fought
in Bastogne under General Patton, marching
three days in the thick of a Belgian winter to break
the famous siege. At home we look up grainy
pictures of the men who survived, the snow-heavy
trees behind them bowed like cranes.
In the photos they are huddled together,
tired as the old men they would become, lighting
damp cigarettes.

FLYING THE PERSIAN GULF

Lord knows he has seen marvelous things,
the night like a room lived in by many people:
ghosts lingering like fathers in a lighted window,
and the sea a ballroom blue with mermaids,
their breasts bright as copper in the sun,
and further down, on the rocky bottom,
the turned-up faces on sunken ships
igniting like tiny moons. He carries

these visions the way some people carry rosaries,
tenderly and without remorse,
and when he says he saw everything but God,
is it because miracles after a while seem
as earthly as diamonds
mined from the black belly of the dirt?

ACKNOWLEDGMENTS

Many thanks to the editors of the journals in which these poems, sometimes in slightly different forms, first appeared: "When the Men Go Off to War," in *Southwest Review*; "Watching from the Runway," in *Poems & Plays*; "A Good Wife before Deployment," in *Prairie Schooner*; "The Messengers" and "Almost," in *Alaska Quarterly Review*; "Planning," in *Chariton Review*; "Quantum Theory," in *North American Review* and *Image Journal*; "The Departure," in *Silk Road Review*; "Standing on the Airfield, before War," in *American Poetry Review*; "Nights in the Gulf," in *Hopkins Review*; "To My Husband, Flying over Afghanistan," in *Nimrod*; "The Funeral," in *Harpur Palate*; "Prayers of an American Wife," in *Georgetown Review*; "On Sundays," in *Cold Mountain Review*; "Kwansaba for a Wounded Warrior," in *South Carolina Review*; "Heroes," in *Southern Humanities Review*; "Outside the Air Base on General Booth Boulevard," in *Main Street Rag*; "The Green Flash," in *Barrow Street*; "Flying the Persian Gulf," in *Madison Review*.

"When the Men Go Off to War" also appeared in *The Best American Poetry 2013*, edited by David Lehman and Denise Duhamel (Scribner, 2013), and was made into a short film for Motionpoems Season 5 by filmmaker Noah Dorsey.

Additionally, the following poems appeared in the chapbook *Prayers of an American Wife*, published by Autumn House Press (2013) and co-winner of the Coal Hill Chapbook Prize: "When the Men Go Off to War," "The Messengers," "Almost," "Kwansaba for a Wounded Warrior," "To My Husband, Flying over Afghanistan," "Standing on the Airfield, before War," "The Green Flash," "The Funeral," "Nights in the Gulf," "Planning," "On Sundays," "Prayers of an American Wife," "Atlantic City," and "The Departure."

I am indebted to my many friends and mentors for their support of my writing over the years: my fabulous agent, Trena Keating; Dick Allen; Todd Boss and the Motionpoems team; Kevin Brockmeier; Geraldine Brooks and Tony Horwitz; Connie Brothers, Deb West, Jan Zenisek, and the Iowa Writers'

Workshop; Ethan Canin; Sarah Cantin; Edward Carey; Sam Chang; Leo Damrosch; Gerald Dawe, Deirdre Madden, Jonathan Williams, Lilian Foley, the late E. A. Markham, and the Trinity College Dublin Creative Writing Program; Kwame Dawes; Noah Dorsey and Heather Beatty; Jennifer duBois; Jehanne Dubrow; Denise Duhamel; Jose Falconi; Jerry Hendrix; Luisa Igloria; Joan Jakobson; Michael Khandelwal, Lisa Hartz, and the Muse Writers Center; David Lehman; Erin McKnight; Jim McPherson; Keija Parssinen; Dee Rincon; Marilynne Robinson; Tim Seibles; Michael Shinagel; Michael Simms, Guiliana Certo, and Autumn House Press; John Stauffer; Tony Swofford; Trina Vargo, Mary Lou Hartman, and the U.S.-Ireland Alliance; Katherine Vaz. Thanks also to Laura, Lyndsey, Kelly, Gavitt, Stacey, Kate, Liz, Mallory, Lizz, Eric, Lea, Rob, Austin, Josh, Loren, Jason, Jessica, Alyssa, Sheena, and Eric, for more than a decade of friendship; and to the wonderful wives of Virginia Beach who inspired this book, of whom there are too many to name but whose friendships I cherish.

Finally, tremendous gratitude is due to the Naval Institute Press for taking a chance on this book, especially my wonderful editor, Gary Thompson; and to my family—Mom, Dad, Christine, Eric, Laura, Marie, Jim, Chris, Jay, Carolyn, Hank, Josie, Arleen, and Farrell. And to Will, for his love and for our daughters—the greatest gifts of all.

ABOUT THE AUTHOR

VICTORIA KELLY is a graduate of Harvard University, the Iowa Writers' Workshop, and Trinity College Dublin. Her fiction and poetry have appeared in *Best American Poetry 2013* and renowned literary journals such as *Alaska Quarterly Review, Southwest Review, Prairie Schooner, North American Review,* and *Hopkins Review.* Her poetry chapbook, *Prayers of an American Wife,* was published by Autumn House Press in 2013. She lives in Virginia.

ML   12-15